THIS BOOK BELONGS TO:

_____

WELCOME TO NEW YORK

Dedicated to Mickey M.

All rights reserved.
No part of this book may be reproduced in any form or by any means, electronic or mechanical, and no photocopying or recording, unless you have written permission from the author.

ISBN 978-1-958985-45-8

Text copyright © 2025 by Mimi Jones

www.joeysavestheday.com

A Mimi Book

New York was named in honor of the Duke of York, who later became King James II of England.

New York was the eleventh state to join the Union. It officially joined on July 26, 1788. It is one of the original 13 colonies.

New York is situated in the Northeastern region of the United States and is bordered by five states: Vermont, Massachusetts, Connecticut, New Jersey, and Pennsylvania.

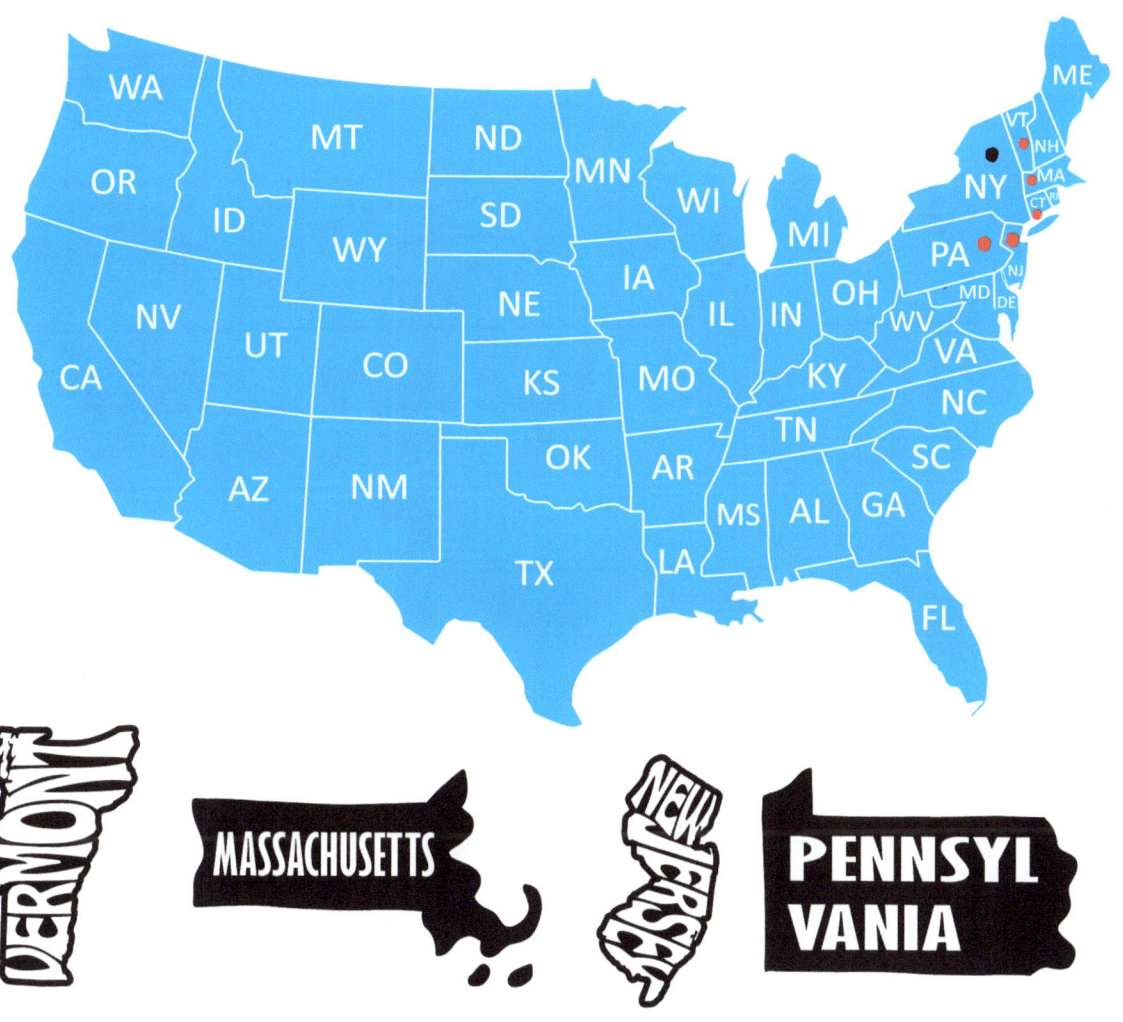

Albany, a city located in the state of New York, officially became the capital in 1797.

Albany, New York, has an estimated population of around 96,860 people.

New York is the 27th largest state in the U.S. and is considered a relatively large state.

New York State Capitol
4 State St
Albany, NY 12207-2804

Walt Whitman was born in 1819 on Long Island, New York. Known as the father of free verse, he is one of New York's most celebrated poets. His work, especially "Leaves of Grass," revolutionized American poetry.

The Brooklyn Bridge, which opened in 1883, connects Manhattan and Brooklyn across the East River. The bridge was designed by John Augustus Roebling and was completed by his son Washington and daughter-in-law Emily.

There are 62 counties in New York.

New York

Here is a list of twenty of those counties:

Dutchess	Orange	Madison	Tioga
Franklin	Queens	Jefferson	Sullivan
Livingston	Rockland	Columbia	Washington
Kings	Warren	Oswego	Yates
Niagara	Monroe	Seneca	Hamilton

In 1886, the Statue of Liberty was gifted to the United States by France. The statue stands in New York Harbor as a symbol of freedom and democracy. It was designed by Frédéric Auguste Bartholdi and engineered by Gustave Eiffel. The statue, including its pedestal, stands 305 feet tall. Originally copper, its color has slowly turned green over time.

The Twin towers were two tall buildings in New York City that were a part of the World Trade Center. Each Tower had been 110 stories high and were made of steel and glass. People from all over the world had worked in the offices inside the Twin towers. On September 11th, 2001, terrorists had attacked New York City by crashing planes into the Twin Towers causing both to fall.

The 9/11 Memorial in New York City honors the nearly 3,000 victims of the terrorist attacks. The memorial features two large pools with waterfalls where the Twin Towers had once stood. The names of everyone who died are inscribed around the pools.

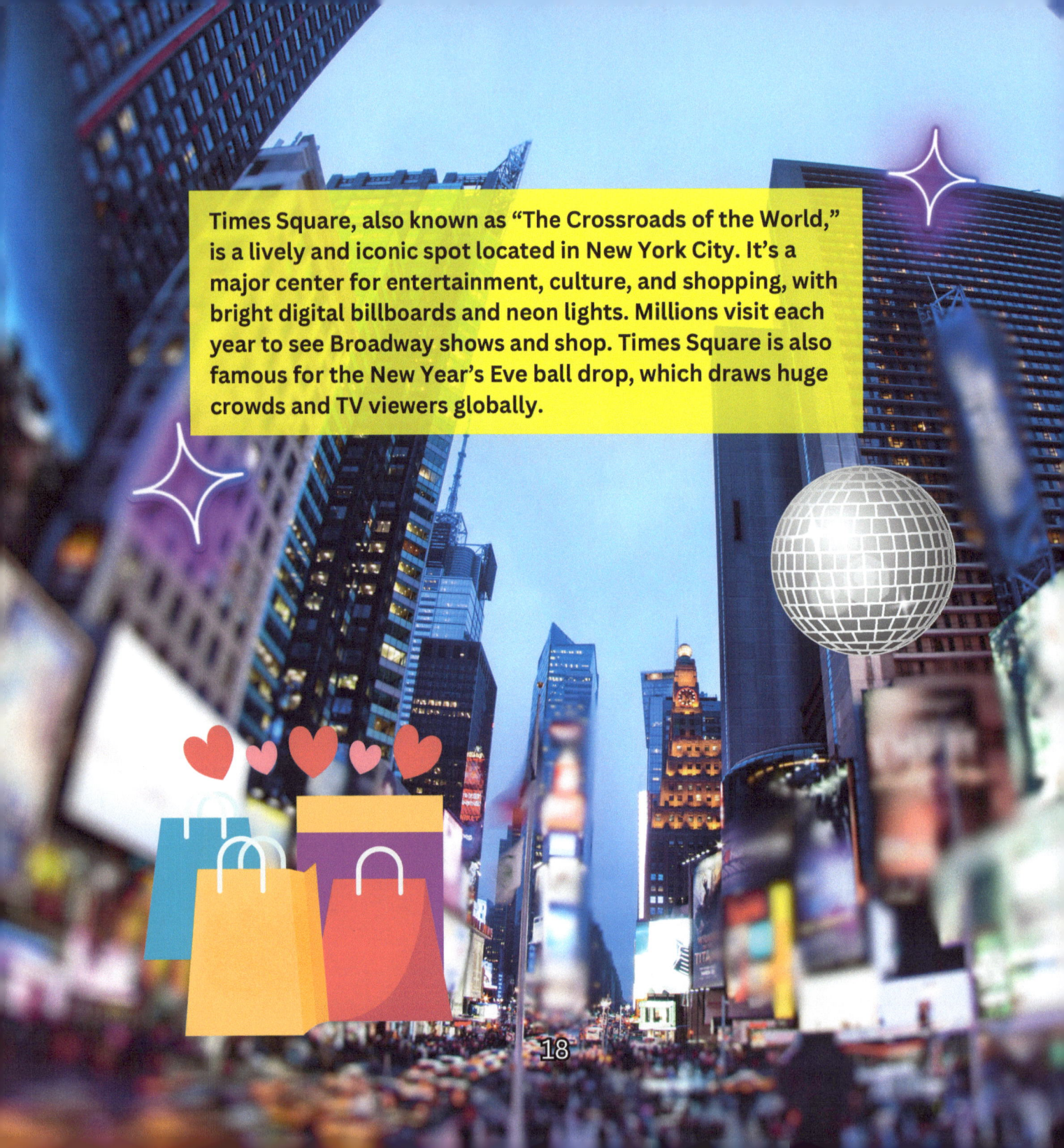

Times Square, also known as "The Crossroads of the World," is a lively and iconic spot located in New York City. It's a major center for entertainment, culture, and shopping, with bright digital billboards and neon lights. Millions visit each year to see Broadway shows and shop. Times Square is also famous for the New Year's Eve ball drop, which draws huge crowds and TV viewers globally.

New York's state bird is the Eastern Bluebird it was chosen as the state bird on May 18, 1970.

The official state flower of New York is the rose. It was chosen as the state flower in 1955.

Some popular nicknames for New York include the Empire State, the Big Apple, and the City That Never Sleeps.

Empire State

The Big Apple

The City That Never Sleeps

The New York state motto is Excelsior. The motto is a Latin word that means "ever upward." The New York state motto was officially adopted in 1778.

The abbreviation for New York is NY.

NY

The current design of New York's state flag was officially adopted on April 1, 1901.

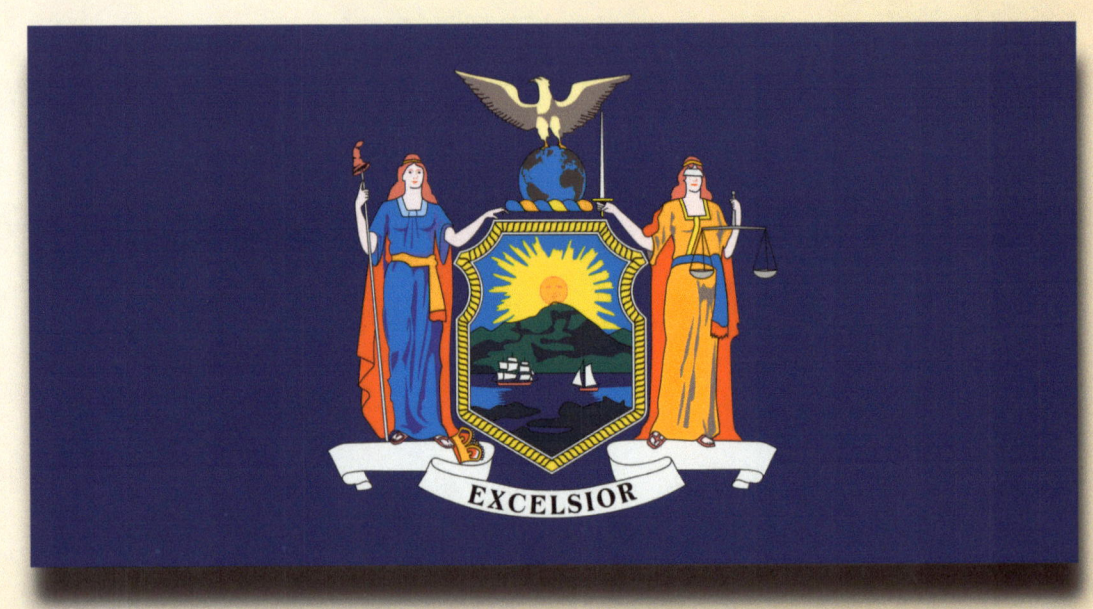

New York boasts a wide array of crops that flourish in its diverse climates and fertile soils, including apples and cherries.

New York can get very hot and cold depending on the time of year. The hottest temperature recorded was 108 degrees Fahrenheit in Troy, on July 22, 1926 and the lowest was -52 degrees Fahrenheit in Old Forge on January 18, 1979.

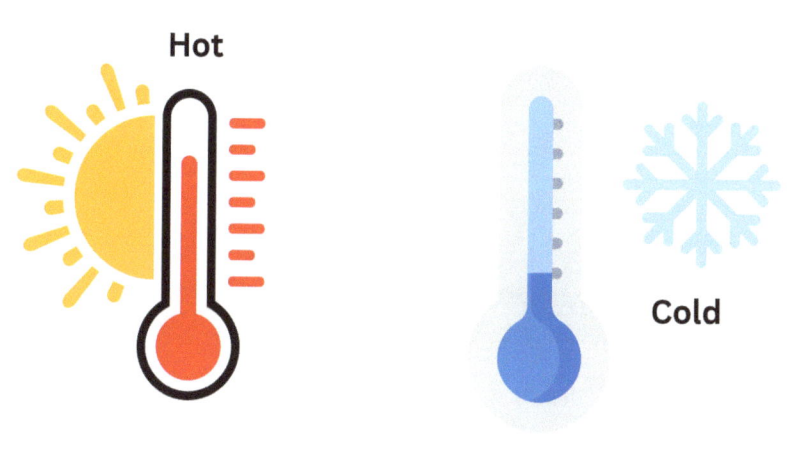

Central Park is a vast, green escape in New York City, designed by Frederick Law Olmsted and Calvert Vaux. Covering 843 acres, the park offers many activities such as jogging, picnicking, and boating. Central Park also has attractions like the Central Park Zoo, the Conservatory Garden, and Bethesda Terrace.

The Empire State Building, completed on May 1, 1931, is located in Manhattan and stands at 1,250 feet tall. Once the tallest building in the world, it has 102 floors that offer breathtaking views of the city.

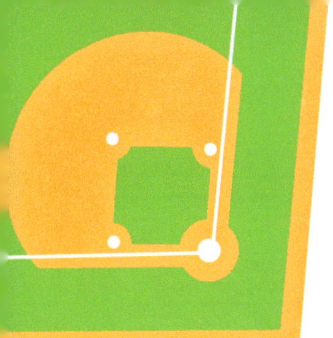

The New York Yankees, based in the Bronx, New York, are a Major League Baseball team founded in 1901. They are one of the most successful franchises in baseball history, with 27 World Series championships. The Yankees play their home games at Yankee Stadium and are known for their iconic pinstriped uniforms and dedicated global fan base.

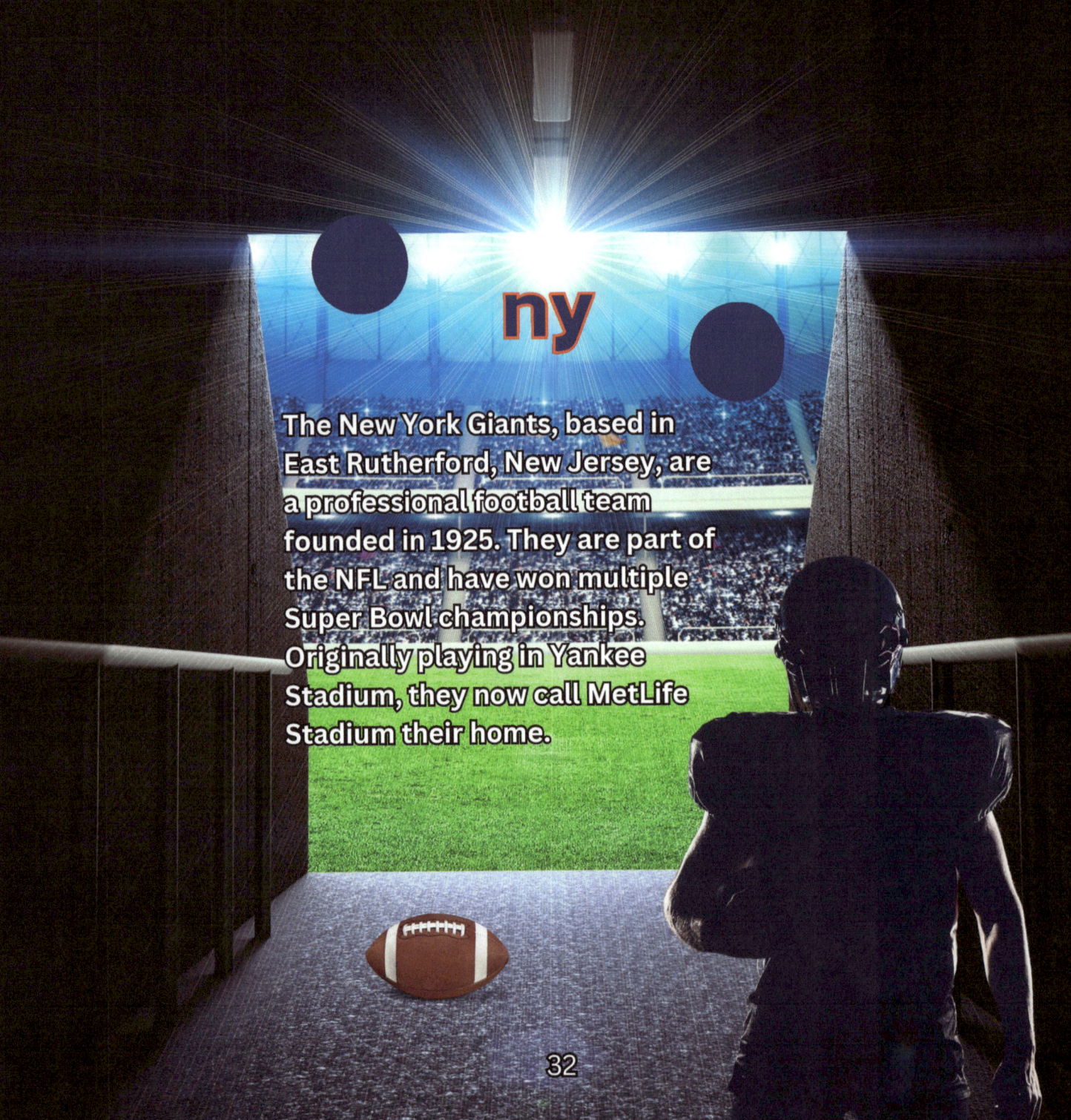

ny

The New York Giants, based in East Rutherford, New Jersey, are a professional football team founded in 1925. They are part of the NFL and have won multiple Super Bowl championships. Originally playing in Yankee Stadium, they now call MetLife Stadium their home.

Niagara Falls, located between the U.S. and Canada, is a stunning natural attraction. It consists of three waterfalls: Horseshoe Falls, American Falls, and Bridal Veil Falls. It's a popular spot for tourists, offering boat tours, observation decks, and scenic parks. It is a must-visit for anyone in New York!

Born in 1856 in Smiljan, which was part of the Austrian Empire, Nikola Tesla emigrated to New York in 1884. As a famous inventor, he is best known for creating the induction motor and many other groundbreaking inventions.

Can you name these?

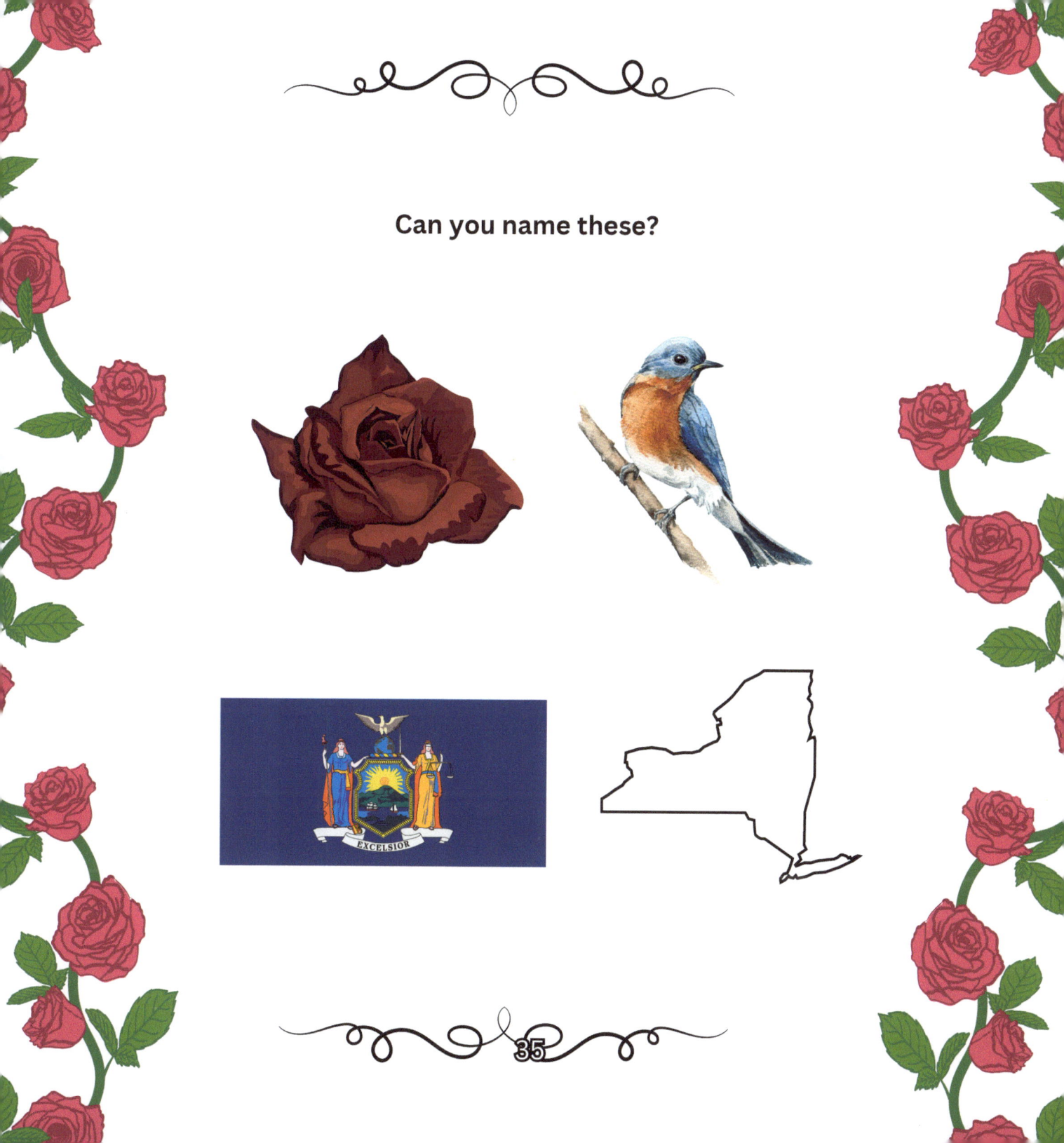

I hope you enjoyed
learning about
New York.

To explore fun facts about the other 49 states, visit my website at www.joeysavestheday.com. You'll also find a wide variety of homeschool resources to support joyful learning at home. If you enjoyed this book, I would be grateful if you left a review. Your feedback truly helps. Thank you for your support!

Check out these other interesting books in the 50 States Fact Books Series!

www.mimibooks.com

www.ingramcontent.com/pod-product-compliance
Lightning Source LLC
Chambersburg PA
CBHW040028050426
42453CB00002B/41